Water, Water Everywhere

Water, Water Everywhere

Mark J. Rauzon and Cynthia Overbeck Bix

Sierra Club Books for Children • San Francisco

The Sierra Club, founded in 1892 by John Muir, has devoted itself to the study and protection of the earth's scenic and ecological resources—mountains, wetlands, woodlands, wild shores and rivers, deserts and plains. The publishing program of the Sierra Club offers books to the public as a nonprofit educational service in the hope that they may enlarge the public's understanding of the Club's basic concerns. The Sierra Club has some sixty chapters in the United States and in Canada. For information about how you may participate in its programs to preserve wilderness and the quality of life, please address inquiries to Sierra Club, 730 Polk Street, San Francisco, CA 94109.

First Paperback Edition

Library of Congress Cataloging-in-Publication Data

Rauzon, Mark J.
    Water, water everywhere / by Mark Rauzon and Cynthia Overbeck Bix. —1st ed.
        p.   cm.
    Summary: Describes the forms water takes, how it has shaped Earth, and its importance to life.
    ISBN 0-87156-598-6(hc)
    ISBN 0-87156-383-5(pb)
    1. Water—Juvenile literature. [1. Water.] I. Bix, Cynthia Overbeck. II. Title.
GB662.3.R38 1993
551.48—dc20   92-34521

Book and cover design: Bonnie Smetts
Printed in Singapore
10 9 8 7 6 5 4 3 2 1

for Suzanne
and all the little raindrops everywhere

— M.J.R.

Earth, the water planet,

shines brightly in the blackness of space.

White clouds swirl all around it,

over oceans of deepest blue.

Water brings color and life to the earth.

Without it, our planet would be

dusty, dry, and dead.

Water is everywhere.

It washes the sky with rain

and rushes along in rivers.

It splashes down waterfalls

and sparkles in the dewdrops

caught on a spiderweb.

Water is part of every living thing.

The stems and leaves of plants,

the bodies of humans

and other animals —

all are made mostly of water.

Water changes its form
almost like magic.
When water is a liquid,
we can spray it from a garden hose
or watch it trickle down the windowpane
during a summer shower.

When water is boiling hot,
it produces droplets called steam,
which we can see whistling
from the spout of a teakettle
or erupting from a hot spring
deep underground.

When it gets very cold,
water freezes into solid ice.
It may be as big as an iceberg
floating in the Arctic sea
or as small as the ice cubes
tinkling in a glass of lemonade.

The water on earth now

is the same water that was here

when earth began.

Water changes its form over and over

in a never-ending cycle.

It rises into the air

from oceans and lakes

as vapor, a gas we cannot see.

As it rises, the vapor cools

and turns back into tiny water droplets,

which form clouds.

As the clouds drift across the sky,

the droplets stick together

and fall back to earth as rain.

If the air is very cold, the rain freezes

and falls as hail, sleet, or snow.

Some of the rain and melting snow

soaks into the soil

and goes deep into the earth.

Some of it flows back

into rivers, lakes, and oceans.

Sooner or later, the same water

will turn into vapor again —

and it will begin its journey once more.

The movement of water

from the earth's surface

to the air

and back again

is a cycle that will go on forever.

Water is always moving

over the land, too.

A mountain spring

bubbles up out of the earth

and rushes down a mountainside.

On its way to lower ground,

the water splashes around rocks

and tumbles over waterfalls.

Farther down the mountain,

the little stream joins with others

to form a small river.

As more streams and rivers empty into it,

the current grows deeper and wider.

The river flows on over the land

until at last it meets the sea.

As water moves, it shapes the earth.

The muddy water of rivers

works like sandpaper.

Over millions of years,

it wears away solid rock,

cutting canyons deep into the earth.

High in the mountains

and in the coldest parts of the world,

snow builds up to form

deep fields of ice called glaciers.

As they slide slowly downhill,

glaciers pick up rocks and boulders

and, over thousands of years,

gouge out great valleys.

As ocean waves batter the shore,

little by little

they break down

the rocky cliffs

and grind them into sand.

Wherever water travels,

it brings the gift of life,

for all living things depend on water.

Trees and other plants grow thick

along waterways and beside lakes.

Rain helps keep forests and gardens

lush and green.

Thirsty animals drink their fill

and splash in cool water holes.

Some creatures,

like lobsters, fish, and whales,

spend their whole lives in water.

People depend on water, too.

We need clean, fresh water to drink,

and the basic foods for everyone on earth

need plenty of fresh water to grow.

People use water in many other ways.

We use it for cooking, washing, and bathing.

We use it to help make electricity

and to put out fires.

Water is also a handy "highway."

On boats of all kinds,

from dugout canoes to huge tankers,

people travel and carry goods

from place to place.

Because people depend on water,

we build our towns and cities

near lakes, rivers, and bays.

Water covers almost

three-fourths of the earth,

but nearly all of it is salt water.

Only a very small amount is fresh water —

and most of *that* is frozen in glaciers

near the North and South Poles.

The tiny bit of fresh water

that is not frozen

supports much of the plant

and animal life on earth.

Because we have such a small
supply of fresh water,
and because the number of people
who use it keeps growing,
we must learn to use our water wisely.

People waste water every day,
often without realizing it —
when we don't fix leaky faucets,
when we leave the water running,
when we take baths
instead of quick showers.

In many places, people are using water
faster than it can recycle itself.

We must also learn
to keep earth's water clean.
Cities dump tons of
waste into the ocean.
Factories empty harmful chemicals
into rivers, lakes, and bays.
Smoke from cars and industry
mixes with water vapor in the air
and falls to earth as acid rain.

All these things
pollute our water supply,
making it too dirty for people
and other animals to drink,
and too dirty for fish
and other creatures to live in.

Polluting our planet's water

spoils not just its usefulness,

but the beauty it brings to the earth.

We love to watch a clear lake

sparkling in the sun.

We tingle with the feel of cool water

flowing over our skin as we dive in.

We delight in catching

snowflakes on our tongues

and in skimming down

snowy mountain slopes on our skis.

We pause to hear the music

of a bubbling forest stream

or to breathe in the fresh,

salty smell of the sea.

Being near water

keeps us in touch

with the life of the earth.